THE 7 PERCENT

Mindset

Survive and Thrive in the Face of Adversity

by

MICHAEL DUCILLE, JR.

Table of Contents

Preface

To me, publishing a book was the sign of an accomplished person. It meant they had achieved a level of success that other people wanted to read about so they could follow in their footsteps. It meant they had enough depth and significance to actually fill an entire book with words that motivated and inspired people to make changes in their lives in pursuit of a different reality. Deep down, I wanted to know what that felt like – to write my book, a book that would inspire others, using my own experience. But truthfully, I wasn't entirely sure that I had the capacity to formulate enough words to write this book – let alone, words that would resonate with people in a way that was actually meaningful and encouraging.

The dream of writing a book was never about fame. I simply wanted to help as many people as possible, in the most efficient way possible. I wanted to reach people that I might never get the chance to personally meet in my lifetime. One thing I know for sure is that we are all given a voice - a sound that we can release into the world that someone, somewhere needs to hear. We are all given the ability to use our experiences, both good and bad, to help someone else and encourage them in whatever they might be facing.

Someone is needing us to breakthrough first, so they'll have the faith and belief to breakthrough too. We might not handle every situation perfectly, but people learn from our wins and losses, from our success and failures.

I know that God gave me a talent for speaking. I also know that He expects me to carefully steward what He's given me because that is how the talent grows and that is how people are positively impacted. If I don't use my gifts, then I'm not only doing a disservice to myself, I'm doing injustice to those people who need to hear my sound.

And the same is true for you. There are gifts, abilities, and talents that you've been given by God (or the universe or higher power - or whatever you believe in) that no one else has. No one else on this planet has your unique combination of strengths and abilities, and there is someone out there who needs you to release what you've been entrusted with.

I know it may be hard to imagine that anyone out there is waiting on you, but the truth is - they are. And if you allow fear to keep you from telling your story or sharing your gift, then the people you were created to impact will miss out on being blessed by you.

Think about all the people who have positively impacted your life. Where would you be today if they had let their insecurities keep them from using their gifts? Are you willing to allow others to be robbed of their blessings because of your insecurities, or the fear of being different or talked about? People are going to talk about you anyway, I say, be proactive and give them something awesome to talk about.

Now, enough about you – back to my story! Once I committed to using my gifts and releasing my sound into the world, it still took a while before my hard work started to pay off, but once it did, things happened quickly. After less than a year of The 1 Percent Mindset being founded, I released my first motivational album titled "The 1 Percent Mindset Presents: You vs. You". And a few months after my album, I published my first book – all within a year.

I had no idea that my material would encourage and inspire people in the way that it has. I still receive text messages, even 6 months after the fact, from people saying how much the album has impacted them.

But to be completely honest, no one becomes a success on their own – we all need help. And I had an amazing team of people who worked around the clock to ensure the success of everything I've put out so far. From my very first videos to my social media campaigns, the motivational album and even this book that you are now reading.

I couldn't have done any of this by myself and I am so grateful for the people that rallied around me, supported me and gave of their time to sow into my dreams until many of them became realities.

Although I didn't achieve this success alone, I had to keep myself motivated enough to put in the hard work and make the right connections to find the right people who could support me on this journey.

A lot of times, I had to go into isolation mode and have a serious reality check with myself. I had to confront my weakest areas and enlist the help of the people in my circle to do the things I honestly couldn't do. While I have a lot of strengths and gifts, I'm far from perfect and there's a lot that I cannot do – and if you're anything like me – you are extremely grateful for the people in your world who are strong in the areas that you are not.

I have been extremely blessed to find some amazing people who were willing to support me along the way. And, I know it seems cliché for a person to thank their mother, but my mom supported me through every step of my journey so far. Regardless of what I had set my mind to, my mother was always there for me. From starting my first business selling lotions and potions to joining my fraternity, my mother supported me – even driving over 3 hours to see my probate show when I crossed into my fraternity. She was always there, supporting me, loving me, encouraging me and challenging me. She always encouraged me to live to my fullest potential. She was faithful in reminding me of the greatness that I had within and that the only person that could stop me from living out that greatness was me. A lot of my work ethic comes from the example that my mother set. She always did whatever she needed to do in order to provide for our family. I remember when she worked two full-time jobs while also going to school full-time. And whenever I start to complain about being stressed or tired, I remember all the hard work and long hours she put in to provide for us and better herself and that always provides a perspective shift. To me, she is the true definition of Superwoman. She did what she needed to do with such grace and she never complained. She never took her stress out on us or made us feel bad for the life she was fighting to give us. I owe everything I am to her and the example that she has set for me, and I intend to continue to work hard and make her proud.

Now, I don't want to give the impression that my dad wasn't present in my life. He was a very prominent figure in my world and still is to this day. I was fortunate enough to grow up with both parents for the majority of my childhood before they ended up getting divorced. Often times as kids, we don't fully appreciate who our parents are or what they do for us, but as I grew up, I came to understand how strategic and hard-working my father really is.

And in addition to being one of the handiest of handymen I know, my dad was very intentional about his relationships – who he allowed into his inner circle and what he opened up about. He taught me that everyone can't be trusted and not everything can be shared with everyone.

He was calculated in everything he did and one of the most valuable lessons that he taught me was that trust is always EARNED, not given.

He taught me that not everyone who claims to be a friend will have your best interest at heart, no matter how long you might have known them. People can hide their true feelings for a long time, but once they show you who they really are – believe them.

He also taught me that jealousy and envy are real things and that I always needed to be mindful of the wolf in sheep's clothing. There are always people who are willing to be your friend while you're on the same level as them, but once you start to move up and do better, their emotions take over and instead of supporting you and doing better themselves, they try to take you out. Beware of those "friends".

While I've had a lot of highs and lows throughout my life, I know that I am the person I am today because of the life lessons I've learned from my parents and friends, both real and fake.

Before moving onto the first chapter, I just want to say a huge thank you to everyone who has, directly and indirectly, influenced my life and in this process. I owe you so much more than my words can express, but they'll have to do for now.

I can sincerely say that I would not have had the successes I've experienced so far without each and every one of you playing your part in my story.

Now that you know a little bit about my upbringing, I hope the words and stories that I share in this book will put things into perspective in your own life and help you to walk out your purpose.

I live by the motto, "things happen, so what?" (edited version, of course!). But when you realize that life is going to happen, the days are going to come and go, the minutes are going to tick by on the clock no matter what, you realize you're in control of how your life, days and time are spent. You can choose to spend your time focusing on your problems or you can force each day to serve you and focus on the solutions instead. The choice is yours – the time is going to pass but it's up to you whether it passes successfully or not. And I'm speaking from experience. I made all the excuses in the world to not write this book. I had to take my minutes captive and use my time wisely because I can never get back the time I've wasted – I can only learn how to better use my time to best serve my purpose and the people I was created to help.

One of the biggest encouragements that pushed me to write and finish this book was all the people who, directly or indirectly, liked, commented, texted or called to let me know how my message impacted and inspired them.

So, this book is for you and because of you. With all that being said, let's dive in.

Learn more about The1PercentMindset on:
Facebook: *www.facebook.com/the1percentmindset*
Instagram: *@the1percentmindset.*
website: *www.the1percentmindset.com*

Introduction

Be happy for this moment. This moment is your life.

- Omar Khayyam

Life offers two great gifts; time and the ability to choose how we spend it. When I started to realize how precious life really is, things started to change for me dramatically. I used to say all the time don't stress the unstressable. And for all you literary police out there I know unstressable isn't a word but simply put; not capable of being stressed. There are certain things that will always be constant no matter. I can guarantee you two things, that time will always move and there will always be change. The only constant is change and if I am stressed out with things I can not control then I will always be fighting a losing battle. Once I learned that mentality it became easier, especially during one of my toughest moments in life to date. Cancer.

I have always been relatively healthy for the most part, either running track or in the gym lifting weights. At some point in 2015, I noticed a small elevated lump in my abdominal area but I did not pay much attention to it. Over the course of 2015, I went to multiple doctors who told me don't worry about it, it will go away. The lump didn't hurt at all and quite frankly I never worried about it too much because it never affected my day to day life. Sometime around December 2015, I noticed it was a little sore but only when I touched it. Any other normal activity it seemed fine so again, I did not pay it much attention. I remember speaking to my mother about it and she did what mothers do. My mother told her grown son to get it checked out ASAP. It took a little bit to get it through my head and even with her stern warnings, I still procrastinated until April 2016, when I finally had it looked at. Even at that point when I went to see the dermatologist he told me "this doesn't seem like anything, don't worry about it." I told him I agree but my mom is making me get it checked out so can you please just test it.

Thank God for mothers because a day later I got a call from the doctor's office saying they want to squeeze me in for the next day for emergency surgery. It turns out I had a rare skin cancer called dermatofibrosarcoma protuberans. There are about 1,000 cases a year or 1 in about 1 million people are diagnosed with it. But at that very moment I lived a don't stress the unstressable type of lifestyle. I was scheduled to go out of town that weekend to an amusement park so I asked if I could schedule it for the next week. The medical assistant's voice was shocked but she said yes if you'd like but I really recommend doing it tomorrow. Surgery or theme park passed through my head. I decided to decline her offer and opt for surgery the following week. Theme park here I come, or so I thought.

If I can tell you how real the wrath of a mother is when they are upset. It is very real and the first thing she told me was you aren't going away and you will make the appointment to go tomorrow. What more could I say but 'yes mom' right? I called back and made the appointment for the next day.

Before you make judgement of the situation I want to give you perspective and where my mind was at the time. I was just told I have a rare skin cancer and I would need emergency surgery to remove it. To be honest, I wasn't panicked at all and really didn't think about it much. I figured I have lived with it for an extended period of time already so at this point what is the worst that could happen. I actually planned on playing the lottery because I figured it had to be my lucky day because of how rare the cancer was. If I can get this skin cancer that ultimately affects so few people, my chances of winning the lottery must be great. I shifted my mind from a point of fear and anxiety to opportunity and solution almost immediately. This never took away the severity of what I had but I decided not to let sickness manifest in my head.

Meanwhile, my mom was trying to book a flight to come see me in New York and was worried. I don't have any children so I can not say her thoughts were irrational from a parent's perspective but I was diagnosed with cancer and was less worried than she was. It didn't bother me because I knew one thing for sure was life will happen regardless. I had to focus on the solutions and what was next. I had every right to be upset. I went to multiple doctors and basically was ignored saying it is nothing to worry about. This could possibly have been treated long ago when I mentioned it to the first doctor. However, I didn't feel anything. I was more numb and had a very nonchalant attitude towards the entire situation.

I had a procedure called MOH's surgery that cut the cancer out and I did not have to do chemotherapy or any sort of radiation. MOH's surgery has a 98% success rate so I felt I was in good hands. While I was fortunate, the actual surgery was extremely painful. I'm not sure if it was an option or not, but I was awake the entire surgery and although I was numbed, I felt the deep cuts through my skin. My abdominal area was on fire and after the first cut and testing, there were more cancer cells and I had to go back into surgery for the second time. About 5 hours later, and very fatigued and in pain, I had a successful surgery and was sent home.

Within the first few months, I was back on my feet as normal. But the road to recovery was not easy. I did not realize at the time how much I use my core muscles on an everyday basis. Basic things such as breathing, turning or even lifting my arms was a struggle for me. It made me self-aware of things I took for granted that I assumed will always be there no matter what. I started to recognize what I did have and not focus on what I didn't.

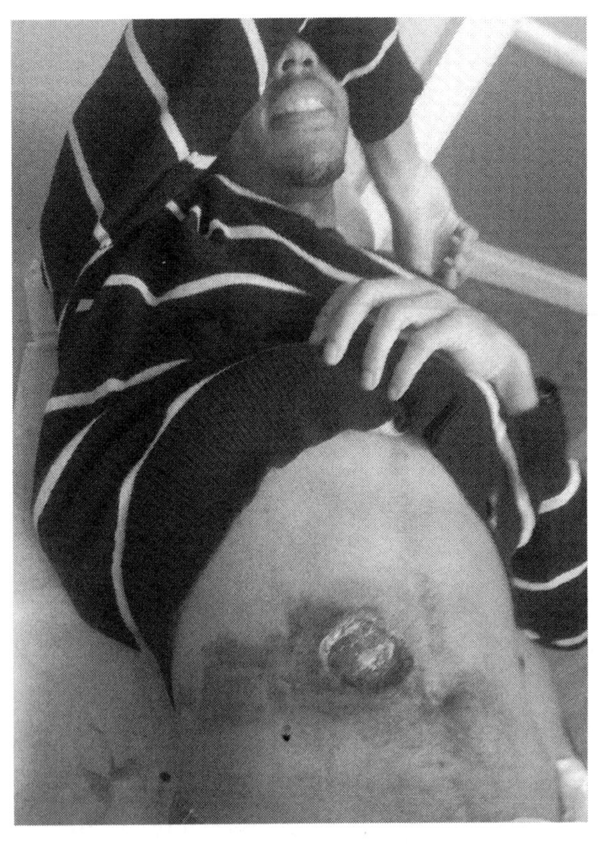

My dad snapped a pic after they cut the cancer out. It looks like I'm smiling but I'm really in a lot of pain. Probably the worst pain I've ever felt in life.

Life humbles you so you can start to appreciate it a little more. I remember walking home from the gym one morning and I saw this homeless man with a McDonald's breakfast sandwich. I'm assuming some kind soul gave it to him. But what I saw next really instilled gratitude into my life where it may have lacked before. Before he took a bite of it, he blessed his food. Something as simple as being grateful for the meal he has despite his circumstance blew my mind. At times we tend to focus on the have-nots but never the haves. I've complained at the most minute things before, but here is someone with no home to go to and never a guarantee of his next meal and he still blessed his food. You don't have to be overly religious to be grateful for what you do have. How many times have you complained about things that won't matter a week from now or even a day from now?

So many things we let control our emotions temporarily that ruins the rest of our day. There are many people who would give their last breath to be in your current situation. And when you practice gratitude, it starts to make life worth living. When you train your brain to experience gratitude from every perspective no matter the situation, you'll naturally reduce stress. Hence why, when I found out I had skin cancer it did not stress me or move my emotions at all. I knew that life could be worse and I still have breath in my body so I have life on this earth. And I am going to live life to the fullest no matter the situation at hand. That's the perspective shift of how one appreciates life. So when situations happen you aren't playing a victim mentality. Lou Holtz famously said, 'don't tell people your problems, 90% of the people don't care and the other 10% are happy you have them." Now, I am not advocating for you to hold everything in and keep things to yourself. What I am saying is do not look for comfort in people. No one can fix your problems but you. But let your situation mold you and use those experiences to learn. Because remember, life offers two great gifts; time, and the ability to choose how we spend it. Make sure you are spending it wisely.

Chapter One

What is The 1 Percent Mindset?

Until I feared I would lose it, I never loved to read. One does not love breathing.

- Harper Lee

The creation of The 1 Percent Mindset all started from doing what most people don't do, and that was to read consistently and started with reading one book per month. According to Pew Research, the median number of books per year the average adult reads is five. I knew if I read just one book per month I was already better than the median. This became a personal challenge in my mid-twenties because I didn't really pick up a book until years later after I graduated college. To be honest, I didn't leisurely read at all and mostly indulged in research-based text for papers I had to write for school. So the challenge began and I started a book club and the goal was to lead the call and make sure the group continued to read at least one book per month. This was my way of holding myself accountable while working on my leadership. It was a fact (based on what my mom told me) that I was more articulate when I committed myself to reading and really diving into books of substance. Books about people who have done amazing things that I look up to and aspire to be like. If you want behind the scenes access to people who have done great things then read about them. It will give you behind the scenes access to everything they went through and how to overcome adversity.

If you want to master your mind, you first have to master what you put into it. The discipline of reading consistently was hard. You have to find consistency and discipline in your life because it is necessary. Discipline is one of the single most important traits of an entrepreneur. You don't become a master in your field without the daily disciplines of trying to master your craft.

I asked many entrepreneurs what does The 1 Percent Mindset mean to them and this answer stood out to me the most:

When I think of the 1 Percent Mindset I believe your mentality is on another level. You are a part of the few that continue to push when things get hard. You believe in true preparation, and you show up when things get hard. Out of 100 people in the room, you're the only one that's showing up to the gym when you don't feel like it. The only one that's willing to take personal responsibility. The only one educating yourself and putting yourself in the best possible situation to win.

You embrace adversity and get motivated when the challenges come ahead. Because you know, it's all a part of the journey.

When I think of The 1 Percent Mindset, I think of people who are elite in their particular field or line of work. It is never money based although the consequence of being elite typically determines your income level. When you are widely considered the best at anything you have to account for the discipline and level of commitment it took to become that person. Discipline by definition is activity, exercise, or regimen that develops or improves a skill; training. The operative word for me is activity. Sometimes the hardest thing to do is start but once you start it is to stay consistent. When you are disciplined it doesn't matter what the excuse is, you will find a way to get it done. The idea is to improve on a skill. **LeBron James**, widely considered the best basketball player on the planet, has secured his bid to the National Basketball Association Hall of Fame. But what makes him great isn't just his God-given ability, but his work ethic. LeBron's desire to be great stems from his constant mental push and expectations of himself. He speaks about working out 5-7 days a week just to make sure he stays in the best shape at all times. In the off-season, when players are resting up, he gets up at 5 am to work out so he can stay in shape throughout the year. The discipline to do that during the off-season for many would be difficult. After the 9-month long basketball season, the last thing players think about is getting back in the gym right away.

Most athletes want to rest or take a break. But what separates him is not only his desire to be the best player in the world but to remain there. Athletes showcase their skills for the world to see on a regular basis. If you don't practice your craft no matter your ability you will lose it. I think back to one of the most decorated athletes in Track & Field, sprinter **Usain Bolt**. He holds the world record in the 100m, 200m, and 4x100m relay. His level of dominance was unprecedented and for many years never lost a race he ran. However, after the 2016 Olympics, he seemed to have lost his desire to run. He decided to make 2017 his final season and retire at the World Championships. Throughout the 2017 season, Bolt did not look like himself on the track and he admitted that he didn't love training. The fire wasn't there and it showed at the World Championships where he received a Bronze medal. This does not take away from his dominance during those years but you have to win the mental battle every day to stay on top. Once he lost the fire then the excuses start to take over in your mind as to why you don't want to do it anymore.

The rigor of not only being great but staying great is not easy. There are very few people who have the mindset to continue to strive when times get hard and do what 99% of other people won't do. Someone once told me you aren't unique to problems and the minute you start realizing it, you will become better off. Translation: You aren't the only one going through it so don't get so caught up that life is hard because it is hard for everyone. How you fight through adversity is what will make or break you.

Steve Jobs knows a little about fighting through adversity despite what is thrown at you. When he co-founded Apple in 1976, I am sure he didn't think he would be kicked out of his own company about a decade later after a heated debate with the executive board of Apple. A company you help start up and you are no longer apart of can be crushing to the average person. However, it didn't trip up Steve Jobs much. During his tenure away from Apple he invested and purchased Pixar in the early stages that went on to produce popular movies like Toy Story and Finding Nemo. He also started his own computer company called NeXT and although it didn't do great in sales, Apple went on to purchase NeXT for over 420 million dollars and Steve Jobs returned to the company when Apple needed him most. When Steve Jobs returned he stated, "Apple was on the rocks, much worse than I thought." A man that took a company on the verge of bankruptcy to being the first American trillion dollar company two decades later he is looked at as a leader. His innovation and grit to come out on top is one of the reasons why Apple is where it is today.

So, when you think about The 1 Percent Mindset, I want you to think about all the people who have accomplished great things. But don't just look at their accomplishments, look at what trials and tribulations they faced to get to the level of success they now have. Nothing comes without sacrifice and you have to be willing to give up something in order to obtain the success you desire. Everything great always starts from the shoulders up before the shoulders down. The level of rigor it takes is always unmatched. Your mind will always quit before your body does, so you must strengthen that first. As we dive into some of these principles, I want you to see where you can apply these principles to your life. This mindset isn't for everyone, just a select few. The 1 Percent Mindset! Is that you?

TAKEAWAY

The reason it is The 1 Percent Mindset is because very few people have what it takes to be great. It is so much easier being average so people settle for mediocre because of that. I want you to exercise what it looks like to be great. What character traits are required for you to have The 1 Percent Mindset? The first character trait is discipline. I speak more about this later on in the book but you need to stay consistent even when times get hard. You won't find any successful person without discipline in their lives. The next and sometimes most overlooked character trait is patience. Do you have the ability to put in the work and wait for the fruits of your labor to manifest? You have to give up short term happiness for long term success. Are you willing to work hard for 10 years to get to that one year of breakthrough? Most people quit after a few weeks or a few months so how do you survive 10 years? The success stories of Steve Jobs or Usain Bolt did not transpire overnight, it took time and patience. And last but not least, FOCUS! One of the worst things you can do is lose focus and allow distractions to take its place. Someone once told me successful people do not have time to get distracted. They are laser focused on their goals and what is in front of them. Do not allow the outside world to stop you from achieving your personal best. There will be naysayers and dream killers but having extreme focus will put you one step closer to that goal. Start off by implementing these character traits within your everyday life. Set a goal for yourself and stay disciplined to doing what it takes to achieve it day in and day out. You must practice the art of patience to see if manifest in your life. And be so locked in and focused that nothing will take you away from what is meant to be.

Chapter Two

Mentor

'A wise or trusted counselor or teacher'

- Definition

My First Mentor

Anyone can be a mentor. There are no specific age requirements, job titles, or even socio-economic status requirements to qualify as a mentor. Anyone you aspire to be like, that motivates you in a positive way can be considered a mentor. The purpose of a mentor is to guide you and give you the steps they took to get to where they are and to help you eliminate some of the mistakes they made along the way.

- The first major breakthrough I had was mid-2010 when I met one of my first mentors, Matthew Pitts. At the time, he was the area manager selling life insurance and he was the top sales guy in Tampa, Florida. He knew how to communicate eloquently and reach people in ways I had never seen before.

It was a sight to see and when I finally got into his inner circle the first thing he asked me was what book was I reading? At the time I had been weeks away from graduating with my Bachelor's degree and I did not want to read anything. I actually never read at all unless it was for school. He then said, "I can tell where a man is going by what book he is reading. You can't tell me you want to get better and you aren't personally developing and reading about people who have successfully done it." Even mentors have mentors and if you aren't aiming to get better in life then you will stay stagnant. Or even worse, you'll go backward. Since then, I made it my priority to read at least one book a month minimum. I try to get inside the heads of successful people by reading about the moves they made and how they responded to adversity.

The first major lesson I learned was to listen to your mentors if you aspire to be where they are. Matthew told me to read, and that is exactly what I started to do. There is no point in having a mentor if you are not going to listen to what they say. It is likely they have been exactly where you are now and fought their way to success. If you decide not to listen then you cannot be upset by the results you didn't get because you weren't willing to do the work. There is no magic pill to success. And when indulging in social media, or comparing your life to the next person, it becomes very hard to put things into perspective of the work it takes behind the scenes.

Although my mentorship did not last very long, I gained valuable insight and the biggest takeaway was reading. Over the next few years, I had an entrepreneurial bug and joined many different MLM companies with the hopes of owning my own business and getting rich. Unfortunately, I had little to no success. I was always chasing this dream of what I thought financial freedom looked like. Trying to sell people on this dream of making money and building an empire of people who wanted to sell products and services underneath my team. Because I was chasing the money there was no question that I had little success because it was never a passion of mine. But what it did for me was teach me the importance of personal development. I was personally developing and I even started a book club so my network marketing "team" could grow and develop. I was getting better but I couldn't get everyone on the same page to really build a team. I always had to motivate people to succeed daily and it became exhausting. Zig Ziglar once said *"people say motivation doesn't last. Well, neither does bathing - that's why we recommend it daily".* If you aren't constantly in the business of motivating yourself then it is easy to become discouraged.

In August 2016, I was in a place of stuck. I wasn't getting any worse but I wasn't getting better. I knew that if I wanted to change I needed to be around someone who was doing better than I was. A person that would hold me accountable and help me change my circle and circumstance. Not just someone who was motivating me but someone who was already living their truth. A person who puts in work day in and day out without making excuses or complaining. I reached out to someone who was at the time a six-figure earner in network marketing who decided to walk away to build his own brand. Someone who made zero excuses and lived his life on his own terms. He stepped away from his team and his friends and decided to do things on his terms. I've been working with my friend Anthony for over 2 years and he has pushed me to achieve my personal best.

Jay-Z once said, *"People look at you strange saying you've changed, like you work that hard to stay the same. You're doing all of this for a reason and what happens most of the time is people change. People change around you and start treating you different because of your success."* The first piece of advice Anthony gave me was, be willing to sacrifice everything. If you aren't where you want to be, then there shouldn't be any time for parties, or hanging out. How do you have the time to do anything fun if you are struggling; mentally, physically, emotionally.

There is so much work to do and if you aren't willing to put in the work then there is nothing anyone including myself can do. That message hit home because I never had time but I had time to hang out with friends or do something fun to clear my mind. He had an all work mentality and that was what I needed to whip me into shape. And once you get to the top, you will lose some friends along the way. To do something successful isn't easy and the fact is, the crab in a bucket mentality is real. It is so much easier to tear down other people's building than for them to lay the foundation and build their own.

So, let's examine why people start treating you differently or assume that all of a sudden you've changed when you gain success. Your social herd will be the single most important predictor of your success. Period! Humans are mammals and by nature, we collaborate and that has been the key to human existence for centuries. As human beings, we start to create our own social herds. The question is, are you in the correct social herd? Are the values of your herd uplifting you up to where you want to be or pulling you down to where they are? When you start behaving in a different way than the herd, they will do what is called a correction.

If you look at wolves they hunt in packs and and have a hierarchy. In order to keep the order, everyone has to fall in line. If any wolf does anything that is out of line with the rest of the herd, a warning is sent, typically by the alpha male. If the behavior still doesn't change they will be ostracized from that herd. That is how order is maintained.

As humans, we fundamentally operate in a similar manner with the people we are around. As you start rising above your herd, if they aren't growing with you they'll start to try and course correct. Say subtle things like, "you're too busy for us now. You're big time so you don't have time to hang out with your friends anymore I see." They try and trick you into feeling guilty and that sparks either one of two reactions: You either comply and go back to the herd and stunt your own growth; Or, it stresses you out enough and you realize this herd is no longer serving you and helping your overall growth. When you are not in the correct herd and you start rising, they will try and pull you down. When you are in the correct herd and you fall down, they will pull you back up. Corrections happen all the time in social herds. Either you're in a healthy success-oriented herd that supports your goals or you're in a herd that keeps you distracted all the time when there's work to do.

The power of a mentor is that they will help you course correct to ensure you are a part of the right herd. You CANNOT outrun a bad herd if you consciously decide to run with it. And that was why I decided to hire that mentor in 2016. My social herd was affecting me because they didn't have the same goals in mind. I personally wanted to be an entrepreneur and create my own success and they were comfortable working a job. There is nothing wrong with a job by any means but I always wanted more. I wanted to create and I felt like I could create my own success if I worked hard for me.

Richard Branson once said, *"Entrepreneurs are the crazy people who work 100 hours a week so they don't have to work 40 hours for someone else."* To be honest I never had time to go out or do much. I remember some friends I used to hang with that I had not seen in a pretty long time. One of them said, "hey we would invite you but you don't ever go out so we stopped inviting you." At first, I was offended, but they were right. I was always busy working on something that I never had time to go out. I sacrificed temporary fun for long-term reality. I had to go into isolation mode.

So, Jay-Z's words were true, *"people will look at you strange saying you've changed"*. If you consciously decide that your social group is not elevating you to the level you want to be at, they will then ostracize you because you no longer hold the same beliefs or core values as they do. That resulted in me not being invited out anymore to go out to brunch or to party. But I knew that I needed to hang around people that inspired and motivated me and pushed me to achieve similar goals.

When you have a desire to change your circle, it doesn't mean they are doing anything wrong. I was fortunate enough to have amazing friends who were all career focused and had aspirations and goals in mind. What I didn't have or did not grow up around were entrepreneurial friends. So I knew in order for me to grow and create success and wealth on my own, I had to be around people who understood the struggle of entrepreneurship. People who've had success in that area and could ultimately help me course correct any bad habits or behavior that isn't acceptable within the herd. That was the reason I hired Anthony and he took me under his wing because he lived what he coined as 'The About It Life' and wanted to train me to have the same mindset.

In the next chapter, I will speak about how working with my mentor allowed me to come up with **The 1 Percent Mindset** and what the brand is and will become. But before I get there, I will say it would not have been possible without all of my mentors and being around that good energy. What having a mentor does is save you both time and money to fast track your way to where they are. If they are genuine and really have your best interest at heart, the investment in a mentor is absolutely worth it.

So, I attribute a ton of my success to not only my current mentor/coach but all the mentors I have had throughout my life. I took something from every single person and now I am able to share what I have learned with so many other people. I have been blessed to have my cup filled with great leadership, mentorship and people and it is only right that I pour back into people the same way they poured into me.

TAKEAWAY

Now, the question is what is the best way to find a mentor? There are many ways but whether it was free or paid I took a keen interest in knowing as much about them as possible before I reached out. Take for example Matthew; he was excellent at sales and because I wanted to be as effective, I shadowed him and listened to everything he said. Now, with mentorship, at times there has to be some return on investment. I was on Matthew's sales team so my development and making sales helped him make money. I was under his wing to get better and ultimately made him more profitable. Although, I did not pay him money directly, he invested his time in me for a return. There are times where you will have to pay for mentorship which I also did with Anthony. I had to invest in myself because I knew it would work out long term later on. You also have to pay people for their value, and as nice as it is to mentor someone for free, I learned it does not always work out like that. The same people you want to mentor you more than likely invested time and/or money on their craft. You will have to pay for the same investment in order to get the returns. There is no cheap way around mentorship if you want to level up. Do not sleep on the value of this chapter because mentorship will really save you years of headaches by eliminating what did not work. The purpose of the mentor is to guide you so you do not make the same mistakes they did. If you find the correct mentor, that should be worth the investment in itself.

Hanging out with my coach Anthony in 2017. He helped me manifest what is now The 1 Percent Mindset.

Chapter Three

Trusting the Process

Sticking to a long-term plan even in the face of bad short-term outcomes'

- UNKNOWN

When I think about trusting the process, it's really about understanding that I need to have the patience to pursue what I'm destined to achieve. The process is never quick or simple. In order for you to appreciate it, you have to work for it. That level of "fight" makes it that much harder to quit when times get rough. It is always your test that creates your testimony.

It took an entire year for the "The 1 Percent Mindset" name to even manifest into what it is today. The journey started because I wanted to hold myself accountable for reading one book a month. I have been a firm believer in reading and what it does not only for the mind but how well I articulate my thoughts to others. Studies show that reading helps with both fluid and emotional intelligence, and so, I made it my duty to be a consistent reader and that's when I decided to start a book club where we tackled one book a month. That December after our book club started, I noticed that people weren't reading consistently and I had to make a decision and figure out how to motivate them.

In the middle of the conference call, I did some research. I know that there are 720 hours in a 30 day month. On average it takes about 6-7 hours to read a book. I'd only be asking for 1 percent of their month. Not their week, not their day, but 1 percent of their MONTH. That message resonated with not only myself but with my readers too because I, myself, wasn't consistent and when I thought about it, all I needed was 1 percent of my month to get through a book. They felt convicted by my message because I was speaking from truth. That message was so powerful that I created a video and put it on Facebook of giving up 1 percent of your month. It must have related to many people because within a day it received over 50+ shares and 4,000 views, even though I didn't have much of a following at the time.

At that point, I realized I had a gift for speaking and inspiring others. Prior to working with my mentor, I had no idea what I was good at or a way to figure out what my gift was. It took about four months of me working with Anthony to realize that I had a gift of speaking. Once that gift was established I created one video a week for the next 11 months on a variety of different topics and received more love and feedback over that year than I could have imagined. That following December my mentor said, *"Yo, you've been giving out free content for the last 12 months, let's see who really supports you. You should come out with a shirt and see who purchases it."*

After running through shirt ideas in my head, that same video I did almost a year prior became a shirt - The 1 Percent: It's A Mindset. Within a few hours, I sold 50+ shirts. I didn't realize how many people truly supported my vision and my message even though they didn't like or share the motivational videos and content I released. It was then that I realized that people are watching you despite what you may think. This was the start of a true testament of what trusting the process really looked like. A year prior to that, no one would have cared to buy my apparel, but over time, they truly came to believe in the vision of "The 1 Percent Mindset". I received many text and messages saying I was their personal mentor or coach without doing anything but speaking truth in a message I believed in.

Here's what I'm telling you: when you are so fixated on your purpose, then it is never about the money. I was doing videos and investing time and money, not even thinking about a return. My sole purpose was to provide value to the marketplace. And when you provide that value, then you become an asset for solving people's needs. Problem solvers become valuable and you will always be paid what you are worth. When you are at the top of your game, you will become an asset and you will be paid top dollars. But you do not figure something like that out overnight, it takes time. Remember it took me four months to even realize I had a gift of speaking and another year after that to come up with the brand name.

Jim Carrey had aspirations to be an actor and through the process, he had to visualize what he wanted. Before he was the Jim Carrey we all know and love, he was an aspiring actor trying to make it. On The Oprah Show in 1997, he spoke about the power of visualization - seeing what you want and then going after it. He would drive in his car and look outside and say that's my car or that's my house. Everything he wanted he would speak life into it. The power behind that was he was broke when all of this was happening. He wasn't where he wanted to be but he knew he wasn't going to stay in the same position. The work that he put in day in and day out to achieve his success was paramount. But before the breakthrough, he went on to say that he wrote himself a check for 10 million dollars for acting services rendered and dated it 3-years out. And in that third year, he received a 10 million dollar check for the film *Dumb and Dumber*. You can visualize it and have faith but without the work, you will remain stagnant. But if you are consistently putting in the work, your mind can take you places you could never imagine.

In order to truly trust the process and fight through the

times that are hard, you have to be fighting for something that you really want. It's easy to get discouraged if you aren't passionate about what you are going after. The lesson behind it is you have to be comfortable waiting, while continuing to push through all the trying times, getting bumps and bruises along the way. I created motivational videos for an entire year without thinking anything of it. I didn't do it for the money or to get speaking gigs, it was something I truly believed I had a God-given ability to do. You have to be willing to play the long game when you're trusting the process, hoping that things will work out as they're supposed to. Is your goal that important to you that you're willing to sacrifice your short-term happiness? Are you willing to give up everything to achieve the dreams that you're after? You start to truly appreciate what you have when you've worked for it. A person that can give up easily is a person who hasn't invested in themselves. When you sacrifice nothing, that's when it becomes easy to quit.

Are you willing to sacrifice and go into isolation mode and trust that what you are doing is the right thing? What does that look like for you? Not partying, sacrificing food or sleep, or maybe even delaying that vacation. There is no success without struggle. You cannot say how bad you want something or desire to achieve success if you aren't willing to give up some of the very basic things required for success. Trusting that doing what can seem like mundane things day in and day out will pay off. It reminds me of an aspiring basketball player who shoots

1,000 jump shots in a basketball gym to perfect his shot. Maybe even an artist who paints without ever knowing if it will sell or not. Or writing that poem you think no one will read or even creating a video that no one may watch. Mastery comes from the art of repetition.

J.K. Rowling, famously known for the Harry Potter series, has an incredible story of perseverance and truly 'trusting the process'. She started writing Harry Potter and within the first 6 months of writing her book, her mother passes away. If that's not bad enough she thought she found love, gets married and has a child but the marriage didn't last very long and now she's a single mother. A single mother and broke living off of welfare she states that she was clinically depressed, but her outlet was in writing. She was determined to finish Harry Potter and when she finally completed the first 3 chapters she sent the manuscript off to a publisher. And another, and another. She was turned down by 12 different publishers before someone finally gave her a chance. Before I go any further, just imagine being a single parent, broke, and trying to pursue your passion of writing and being told "no" 12 different times. The mental space you have to be in to see rock bottom as a foundation, not the ending is incredible. At the point of absolute disappointment and what seems like failure, there is no place to go but up. She used her disappointment as a tool to fund her passion. Now Harry Potter is currently the best selling book series of all time, selling more than 400 million copies. Your failures are the foundation for greatness. You build off of the mistakes you've made to have a solid ground. And those failures and learning experiences take time. You must trust that you are following your vision and pursuing your passion and that eventually, it'll pay off.

Jim Carrey and J.K Rowling aren't unique to adversity but when most people would quit, they found reasons to grow. They didn't want to just survive but they wanted to thrive and live out their dreams. With each hurdle, they continued to trust the process and understood that dedication is always the cornerstone to success. It's the foundational piece of it actually. And once you lay a great foundation, you will trust it withstands the test of time.

TAKEAWAY

When I think of trust the process one of the first things that come to mind is the NBA's Philadelphia 76ers. If you are not a basketball fan bear with me for a second as I put things into perspective for you. Over the last few years, the Philadelphia 76ers have coined the phrase 'Trust The Process to let their fans know it is a painful experience losing now but all will be well in the future. They were one of the worst teams in the NBA for about 4 years, winning only 75 games out of the 328 played. But this allowed them to have the best odds to have the first pick during the NBA draft, and best chance of getting the best players coming out of college. During the 2016-2017 NBA season they made the playoffs for the first time in 5 years by trusting the process. The Philadelphia fans had to endure losing for many years for their team to build a solid organization of the future. During those painful years fans may have said it was not worth it, but how do you think they feel now? If you can fight through the adversity during the painful times then you'll be able to enjoy what is ahead. Eric Thomas once said if you're going through it, what's the point of giving up? Get a reward for your struggle! It is all apart of the process. Which brings me to my next chapter, Adversity!

Met Eric Thomas at the Ignite The Dream tour in Brooklyn.

Chapter Four

Adversity

Adversity causes some men to break; others to break records

- William Arthur Ward

Adversity causes some men to break; others to break records. The beauty of adversity is it will show you exactly what you are made of. My friend used to always tell me pressure bust pipes. But he left out that pressure can also make beautiful diamonds. When you are going through adversity the easy thing to do is to quit. Human nature dictates that when things are hard or when you are tired you stop. But the great ones stop to rest not stop to quit. Most stories of successful self-made millionaires are people who went through hell and back to get to their success. I don't want you for a second to think that you are unique to struggle. I will continue to reiterate it because we tend to think when times are hard we cannot get past it. But the truth is, you can and will if you allow your mind to look adversity as a stepping stone. This is not me saying what you are going through doesn't matter. It is me saying if Jack and Jill can get through it, why can't you? There will always be people who are in worse off situations than you. How did Kyle Maynard with no arms or legs climb Mount Kilimanjaro? How did Oprah Winfrey go from growing up in poverty to becoming one of the wealthiest people in the world? How did rapper 50 Cent go from getting shot 9 times and being a part of the drug world, to becoming a multi-platinum artist and producing hit television shows like Power? These aren't people gifted with special powers but people who had sheer will. When you work hard you don't let adversity become the reason for you to quit.

Martin Luther King, Jr said, "the ultimate measure of a man isn't where he stands in moments of comfort and convenience, but where he stands at times of challenge and controversy." The journey is always easy when you don't have to put in work. It is when you put blood, sweat, and tears into those things that it means the most to you and what makes it hard to quit. You value things more when you have invested in it. Investment of time or money holds weight versus no real investment at all. You start to value things when you have skin in the game so when adversity hits, it becomes hard to give up.

Everyone goes through adversity. As I was building The 1 Percent Mindset Podcast I thought about one of the biggest interviews I had at the time. I just finished reading the book Redefining Strong by Phoenix White (highly recommended) and I reached out to her because I loved her story and wanted her to be on my podcast. Fortunately, she was open to doing the interview with me. I live off of an ask and you shall receive type of mindset and it worked out. I believe interviews are just conversations so when it comes to interviews I typically don't have a precursor of questions that I ask, however, for this big moment I jotted some notes down so I didn't miss any points. Literally 15 minutes before we were scheduled to do an interview I decided to switch from using Zoom video conference to using Google Hangouts. The reason was because I was trying to cut down on my expenses and didn't want to pay for Zoom's premium version that didn't limit conversations to just 45 minutes. I wanted the conversation to be organic and not timed. In my mind that was a great idea and made all the sense in the world to make the switch. And on Google Hangouts you can upload it directly to YouTube. She gets on Google Hangout and immediately my computer starts to freeze and the recording stopped working. I decided to use another program that I found at the last minute and started recording this highly anticipated interview. The interview was phenomenal and Phoenix dropped gems not only for me but for my audience who listens to The 1 Percent Mindset podcast. And of course, my decision to switch made sense because the interview lasted over an hour.

I wrapped up the interview and stopped the screen recording feeling excited about having my biggest guest to date on my podcast. I go to playback the interview and for whatever reason, I can only hear myself ask the questions but can not hear anything Phoenix is saying. I was disappointed in myself for not properly preparing for such an amazing podcast for my audience. But in times of trials and tribulations regardless how big or small, you have to become solutions oriented. People have a tendency to freeze up and not do anything when they are in a place of discomfort. Picture a time when you were the most overwhelmed and think about what you did at that moment. What would your future self-have done differently? For some people, it is as simple as doing something period and figuring out a way to move past the current situation.

So what did I do when that situation happened. For one, I am not going to pretend like I wasn't angry, sad, disappointed all in one. But, the first thing I did was send her a message on Instagram and said: "adversity is an amazing thing". The reality is, it is easy to give someone advice but that much harder to take your own. Someone as busy as Phoenix took some time out of her schedule to book an interview with me. She didn't charge me for her time and I ultimately was not prepared for the situation. I let Phoenix know the situation and she was extremely understanding and because the interview initially went so well, she was fine rescheduling with me. It turns out that our second interview was so much better than our first. Everything happens for a reason and what doesn't break you will always make you stronger. I didn't start writing this chapter on adversity until this situation happened but this wasn't the first nor will it be the last time I will be in a situation that can be highly stressed.

I will give you another story of when adversity kicked me in my butt but I was focused on just the solution. In November 2017, The 1 Percent Mindset was formed and I created t-shirts and hoodies for the very first time. At the time I was very new to t-shirt sales so I reached out to one of my buddies who had a t-shirt line. We worked out a deal where he would create all the apparel orders for me and I just had to send him the money in advance. The money looked great and I thought he did me a huge favor. Being a smart businessman I paid for a few samples so I can make sure the quality of the apparel was good. When it arrived, I was impressed and decided to form a partnership. All I needed to do was give him a spreadsheet of everything and I should be good to go. My first batch of apparel I sent to him was about 40 orders and he told me to give him about a week to do it. The first red flag came when a week went by and there was no communication or shirts sent out. I finally got a hold of him and he apologized and got the first batch of orders out. Instead of it taking a week it took almost three weeks for people to get their shirts. This is the first launch of my new company and I felt completely manipulated by someone I thought was my friend who had my best interest at heart. I didn't have any tracking numbers and I paid him out of good faith through a cash sharing app Venmo. He proclaimed it would never happen again and he will be in communication next go around if he couldn't fulfill on the orders at the time he said he would. The man seemed genuine so I trusted him and took him as a man of his word.

The next batch of orders came in and I sent him money in advance as usual and the same thing happens again. Fool me once, shame on you, but fool me twice then shame on me. I entrusted in someone who said they would fix the situation and this time I had another 30+ order that had to go out and he was nowhere to be found. I sent him multiple text messages and emails trying to get tracking numbers for everything and he completely ignored me. Not only that, I found out he overcharged me for shipping to continue to line his pocket and really didn't do me a favor at all. Multiple people were reaching out to me asking me about their order and I had no idea what to tell them. How could someone take your money that you thought was a friend and completely disappear. The emotion of anger poured through my entire body and I could literally feel myself getting warm. Someone who was supposed to be my friend that I paid all of a sudden went away. Now I know what you are thinking, why didn't you just try and request your money back. Well, I paid him through the cash sharing app Venmo so there is no buyer protection. My advice is when conducting business, regardless of who it is, do it through a company you have buyers protection like Paypal.

At this point, I am pissed off but I couldn't be mad with anyone but myself. He showed me his hand the first time and I still trusted him enough and gave him an opportunity to rectify the situation. I had all these pending orders people paid for, and I paid him for. I decided to go with another company and resubmit the orders. Any profit I did make selling shirts were now reinvested into that second batch of orders because the person I originally used did not deliver on what he said. Did I take a loss investment wise? Yes, but what I gained was knowledge. And that knowledge was priceless so I know the next go around, how to conduct and run a business on my own. You have to be comfortable taking a loss when you're investing because there are no guarantees of success. Anything can happen whether it is bad business or bad marketing but you can't let it deflate you. But I must admit, it can be hard at first. Especially when that person was someone you thought you could trust.

So instinctively I went into defense mode and started to blame the world for transgressions that ultimately cost me hundreds of dollars in profit within a few hours. But in the words of Jay-Z," a loss is not a loss, it's a lesson. Appreciate the pain it's a blessing". After reflection, I immediately stopped blaming myself or anyone else and chalked it up to the game of LIFE. Life has a way of placing you in tough situations to see what you are made of. If you can't handle problems on a micro-level, then you won't be able to handle life on a macro-level. To whom much is given, much is required and the more you are given, the more you will be tested. As you continue to grow you will be tested in ways you would have never imagined, and it is how you get over it that will separate you from the rest. So, play the game to the best of your ability. The game of LIFE.

TAKEAWAY

This is one of my favorite chapters because when I read about the adversity people overcome to make it, I always get inspired and so should you. I have said this before and I will say it again... NO ONE HAS GONE FROM NOTHING TO SOMETHING without experiencing some sort of adversity. There has to be some sort pain whether it be mental or physical to achieve greatness. Think about superhero movies and although fictional it offers a great lesson. There was always some sort of battle a superhero is fighting and usually they start off losing the fight before they win. They overcame adversity and what was in front of them allowed them to become a hero. They know in order to be great you have to embrace the adversity that's ahead and fight through it. There has to be some adversity to overcome for you to win. It is not business if there are not any problems. I will dive a little deeper into Inky Johnson's story later in this book but he said something that will always resonate with me. When faced with my biggest challenge it never mattered because I have been fighting adversity my entire life. The sacrifice, dedication and commitment he made to get to the National Football League immediately went out the window once he became paralyzed in his final season of college football. The blessing in disguise was the amount of people he has been able to impact because of that injury. He speaks about the number of people that became believers of Christ because of his story. Life may not always go according to your plan, but you must always trust his plan. The pain you endure builds character and can also inspire so many others in the process. When adversity hits, just know it is what you need to conquer what is in front of you. Continue to train your mind to fight through those trying times.

Chapter Five

Health is Wealth and also Discipline

If you look good, you feel good. If you feel good, you play good. If you play good, they pay good.

- Deion Sanders

Athletes are some of the most structured and disciplined people that you will ever meet. The committed ones at least. At a very young age, my parents had me running track and cross country year round. Even if I wanted to, I never had time to get into any trouble because I went from school to practice to school to track meets. I had no time to do anything but what was required. Once I got a little older I stopped training and my structure changed. I was no longer required to go to practice and wasn't disciplined enough to keep my health in tact let alone anything else in my life. The foundation that was left for me went out the window when I was given free will.

Being a fairly slender guy my entire life I never had to worry about gaining weight or being obese. That was probably one of the reasons I stopped training all together. In my late 20's I noticed walking up stairs I would be out of breath. I'm 20+ slender guy and had trouble breathing walking up flights of stairs. I immediately knew I had to make a change so I decided to do what I knew best. Run!

I signed up for the Brooklyn Half Marathon about 5 months prior to the race and I set a goal to run it under 2 hours. At this point I am well over a decade removed from running or anything physical. I never ran anything more than 6 miles straight in my life, and I am in New York, in the dead of winter, with abysmal temperatures. But I knew if I wanted to make a change in my fitness and health then it comes with sacrifice. Over those 5 months I teamed up with my old track coach and I trained at least 5 days a week. Whether it was 20 degrees or 80 degrees I made time to run. I set a time goal and had high expectations to complete it in the time I said I was going to. Failure wasn't an option for me and if I did not make the time I knew I gave it everything I had to complete it. What I did have a problem with was not taking it seriously and being comfortable not hitting my goal. I had a big problem not reaching the time knowing I didn't give it my best shot. So I was committed to do everything I could to get it done. I spoke life into my goals and told the world not only to hold me accountable but for the world to hold me accountable as well.

I trusted my training and preparation and up until a week before the race I come down with a fever. I had the flu for the entire week leading up to the race and only thing I did was drink water and try to sweat it out. Race day comes and I still had my goal in mind and did not want to make excuses as to why I can't but focused more so on why I could. I exceeded all expectations and my official time was 1.47.53. I had over 12 minutes to spare even being half sick. I didn't want to use sickness as an excuse so I gave it everything I had until the finish line. I will admit, it wasn't easy and I was almost walking when I crossed the finish line. My sickness got the best of me with about 3 miles to go but the mission was always in the back of my head.

I was proud of my accomplishment and decided to run the same race the following year after a push from my friend. I didn't attach any running goals to it because at this point I was in the gym working on getting bigger so I didn't do much cardio. Literally, a month before the race I decided I should start running to get ready for this race. The first day training, I hurt my achilles and wasn't able to train at all leading up to the race. I did some therapy to try and lessen the load because the goal was to still run it and I had about a month to make it heal. It was almost like dejavu because I got sick again. This time my sickness was worse than I was last year. The night before the race I am up coughing my lungs out with only a few hours before I have to get up for the race. I am wondering if it is even worth running this race. The weather was terrible that day. It was raining and cold and I had every excuse to not do it. But I made a commitment to myself that I am going to give it everything I had. I won't jeopardize my achilles but even if I had to walk the entire way, I will finish the race. And that is exactly what I did, I finished the race and still did it with a reputable time. Snot coming down my nose, and chills but I dragged myself across the finish line because it meant more to finish than to quit. So with every thing I had left in my body, I finished.

At a young age, I was always taught, if you don't know how to lose, then you will never know how to win. My coach used to say, "I don't care if you are first or butt-naked last, you will finish the race and you will do it with pride". That life lesson always stuck with me because it shows the ultimate measure of a man. No problem enjoying the praises when things are good but can you stand with your head held high when things aren't the best? I became an overall better human being when I took defeat pridefully. So, that second half marathon meant so much more to me than the first because I worked 10x harder to finish the race even though the time wasn't as good.

If running isn't your thing then you need to find what physical activity is for you. After my first half marathon

I stepped away from running. I had nothing to push or motivate me to continue my training regimen at the time. I was still creating motivational videos and inspiring people and one of my mentors said you need to get in the gym. And after my first half marathon I made a commitment to get in the gym. He drilled into me how small and sick I looked and I needed to put on weight. In my head I was fine because I've been the same weight since about high school. I was a solid 135 pounds soaking wet. I hated the gym because I was always extremely weak and had no idea what I was doing in there. My pride got the best of me and because I hated the gym I never went. But it was time for a change and a new challenge. I made it a goal to try and gain 15lbs of muscle within the first 6 months. Not only that, I committed to going to the gym every day at 5am when it opened. Not because I had to be there that early, but because it forced me to be disciplined day in and day out no matter what time I went to bed. After 6 months of consistency I reached my goal and have maintained a pretty steady weight since then.

The main takeaway from the gym for me was mindset shift. Adversity/pain/struggle is all mental. You can't avoid thunderstorms but it won't rain forever. The gym forced me to perform at a high level both mentally and physically and trains the mind to adapt and overcome in high-stress situations. I can sit in the room with anyone and no matter their accomplishments or financial situation I can look at someone and mentally know, they don't work as hard as I do. And maybe they do work as hard, but I make it a mission to start my day off with a high-intensity workout. I know hard work beats talent when talent doesn't work hard. Real recognizes real and with my confidence and energy, I have become well respected in any room. But that happened because I took the gym seriously. I noticed not only the physical change but my mental change. I started to inspire people because they saw me consistently at the gym at 5am putting in work. And as Gary Vaynerchuk always says, *"document, don't create."* So that is what I did, I documented everything I did in the physical fitness space to motivate people to take their health seriously. I can't take you seriously if you don't take yourself seriously. If you don't watch the foods you eat or take care of your body, how can I expect you to be of benefit to me? You aren't even of benefit to yourself. If I can impart anything on you from this book, take your health seriously. You are no good to anyone if your body can't function long term. TAKE YOUR PHYSICAL HEALTH SERIOUSLY!

TAKEAWAY

Self-evaluation and being honest with yourself is extremely important. You are evaluating you so do not sugar coat what is in front of you to make you feel better. If you are out of shape do not tell yourself I am not horrible, it could be worse. If you are frail, then hit the gym to get stronger. Before you try to get better for anyone else you have to get better for yourself. I had a friend that looked in the mirror and did not like what she saw. She decided to change her lifestyle and diet because no one could fix her problems but her. She became a vegetarian and remained disciplined with her diet and her health. She lost the weight she wanted and probably exceeded her expectations because of self-reflection. There is now a level of confidence built because not only does she feel good, but she looks great. She is now an inspiration to many other people who thought it was impossible to change their eating habits because of time or finances. She literally gives you zero excuses as to why you can not do it. This takeaway is not to make you feel bad but for you to step into reality of what it takes to be disciplined. What is easy to do is also easy not to do. I made a commitment to do 100 push ups and 100 crunches every night before bed. The entire process takes less than 10 minutes so why is it hard to complete that task on a daily basis? It is because it is so much easier to not do it. Why dread those 10 minutes when I can sit and let the time pass by? That is the difference between someone who kind of wants it and the beast who will go after and get it. You should not have to feel unhealthy inside in order to make a change in your health. It should be natural to make a change to be healthy. But we do it backwards and we wait until something happens to want to make change. When you can be disciplined in your mind and take care of your body you were given, you start to appreciate other areas of life even more. I also challenge you to drink a gallon of water per day for the next 30 days. Up to 60% of the human body is made up of water yet we drink everything but natural water. There are multiple health benefits drinking water such as energized muscles, prevents headaches, and improves complexion. But the discipline required to drink that much water daily with no soda or juice makes for an even better human being. Take on the challenge or drinking a gallon a day and see how it starts to help you not only with your health but keeps you disciplined as well

This was a pic in July 2017 before I started working out. Fast forward a year and in July 2018 I have made fitness a discipline.

Chapter Six

Leadership

A leader is one who knows the way, shows the way, and goes the way

- John C. Maxwell

When I thought about what a leader should look like, or who they represent, some of the greats came to mind. The John F. Kennedy's, Martin Luther King's, and Barack Obama's of the world. Individuals who command attention in any room they walk in no matter what. I can only imagine what kind of power one has when the room is suddenly quiet when you walk in. What kind of personal development and training does one have to go through to really achieve something like that? And when I compared myself to what they've done I never initially thought of myself as a leader. But you don't wake up and become great and/or powerful overnight. There are small microsteps that one must take in order to reach the top of the pinnacle. In order to lead on a large level, you have to first figure out how to be an effective leader in a small setting. Leadership is just the art of motivating people to move towards a common goal or thing; being able to inspire someone to make a decision for the betterment of themselves or the group. It is as simple as that! What that means is, we all have leadership qualities in us. Do not let anyone ever tell you that you can never be a leader. That is simply untrue! I believe that someone is looking up to you right now and waiting for you to finally take that leap of faith and go after your dreams. They are counting on you so they can follow in your very footsteps because you are an inspiration to them. It can be a little brother/sister, friend, acquaintance, whoever. Someone is expecting you to achieve more and is counting on you to make it so you can give them hope. You are not required to speak on a podium in front of millions of people to be considered a leader. Quite frankly, you may not even be a great public speaker, but can lead with your actions and not necessarily your words. It can start with the very foundation of someone coming to you to ask you for advice or how you were able to accomplish a particular task. They trusted enough in you to value your opinion and that is important to understand. So whether you are a CEO of a Fortune 500 company, or starting your first job as a retail sales associate, you can still be considered a leader. You almost have a moral obligation to know that someone is looking up to you right now. They are counting on you to guide them in the best way possible, and you must do right so you do not become a disservice not only to yourself, but to those that look up to you for guidance. It can be anyone and if you do not take your position as a leader seriously, you are essentially affecting someone else. That same person who was waiting for you to start that business and see you succeed so they know it's really possible. That younger sibling who saw you go to college and graduate. Now that becomes normal because you set the standard for them. Your best friend who always admired what you did and saw you go after your dreams of writing a book, or singing in the church choir. The little things you do not see can make the biggest impact on a person.

It was my speaking coach, Koran Bolden who saw something in me and told me it's time to write your book. He spoke to me and said you are a natural and don't waste your gifts. In order to really put your stamp on things and be looked at as an expert in your field, you need to write this book and share your talents with the world. You need to decipher when it is time to be a preacher or a teacher. All leaders have one if not both of those qualities. No one quality is better than the other depending on the audience you have to decide what is most effective.

So, what are the qualities of a leader?

One of the first things I learned as a leader is to be of your word. Effective leadership lives and dies on integrity and without it nothing works. What does it mean for a person to have integrity? A good leader is a person who will get things done no matter the excuse. I need to be able to count on my leader to effectively get the work done they said they were going to do. And not compromise morals or ethics for personal gain. Do not take for granted the power of keeping your word and what that means. You can work for years to gain complete trust and a split second to lose it all. A prime example of this are people who commit adultery in their marriages. A man/woman can work for years to gain the trust of their partner and cheating can ruin it all in the blink of an eye. My brothers, imagine working for years to impress this woman you've had your eyes on and you finally get her attention. You put in work for years and the vows you set are now broken for temporary pleasure. Do not let short term pleasure ruin long term happiness. And the same applies for my sisters as well. For a man to make the decision to make you his wife is a special sentiment. We can't forget that having integrity takes work. It can sometimes mean being uncomfortable or annoyed but you remain true to your word no matter what.

I remember during my childhood years my mom told me to take the meat out of the refrigerator before she got home so it could thaw out. Not taking it extremely seriously I said okay but completely forgot. Now, the effect of my lack of integrity meant when my mother got home the meat was still frozen. Because the meat was still frozen she couldn't cook it after she got off of work. It also meant my behind was in trouble. There was a chain reaction of me not being of my word like being hungry because the meat couldn't start cooking right away. Although it may not seem like much now she lost trust in me whether I wanted to believe it or not. If you can not be trusted to do something as small as taking the meat out the freezer, then why should anyone trust you for anything major. Samuel Johnson said, "the chains of habit is too weak to be felt until they are too strong to be broken." This is such a powerful quote because your integrity will show no matter how big or small the situation is. Your morals and being of your word should not change based on how big or small the situation is. It should just be habit to be of your word. It typically is what you do behind the scenes when no one is watching that defines true leadership.

If you can get really good at doing the little things, then when something major comes up and you have to stand by what you said, it will make it that much easier. Why? Because you are already programmed to get the job done no matter the circumstance or situation. Being honest even if that is admitting you are wrong and have to take full responsibility for your actions. People in power at times never want to look like they are wrong so they try and deflect blame elsewhere. If you are a true leader, you can admit and correct when you have dropped the ball. That is how you build trust amongst the people you are leading. And if you can be trusted and people can count on you no matter what, that is one of the top characteristics that define great leadership. Integrity!

Being an effective communicator takes practice and shows a certain level of confidence a person has. If you break down the art it seems very simple. It is just someone who has the ability to grab people's attention and have them actively listen, understand, and absorb the message you are trying to relay. When you can do that flawlessly you become an effective communicator. I remember going to an event and the speaker said something that will always stand out to me. He said if you can make someone **think, laugh or cry** you will always have their attention. Your words have to be so relatable that you are able to spark one of these emotions. When a movie like *Titanic* comes on, it brings out a human emotion of sadness universally. That emotion releases what is called oxytocin that allows us to feel more connected to the characters. So when Rose in Titanic says, *"I'll never let go Jack"* and releases his hand, you can feel that that emotion of sadness; if you started off a speech with a joke that allows your audience to loosen up and you now have their attention because you made them laugh. Maybe a personal story that explains a tough decision you made, or a particular cause that is near and dear to your heart that you donated to. You can relate to that story and even though it is not your life, your biochemistry allows that connection. If you can build trust in that way by being relatable and understanding that is where effectiveness takes place.

There are many ways to become an effective communicator like understanding tonality. When you need to raise your voice to capture attention or the softer pitch so your audience can understand seriousness. The same leadership a teacher or a parent may have had. I always knew when my parents were disappointed. The tone in their voice made it even worse than getting disciplined. Yes, I have caribbean parents so every now and again, I had a belt to my behind. Of course with lots of love, but the pain of disappointment always hurt so much more. My parents were effective because no matter what they said, they always got their point across. Every true leader can get their point across not only with what they say, but how they say it.

It is imperative that you do not become who I call positional leaders. Those are people who have a particular title that give them leadership roles that they necessarily didn't earn or don't qualify for. Everyone encounters bad leadership or people who just are not very effective leaders, and if you aren't willing to work on it then it will be impossible to effectively lead.

I remember I was working as a recruiter for a company. I switched departments and shortly after the director went on maternity leave for a few months, so a gentleman stepped into the position temporarily to fill that leadership void. Immediately we bumped heads and we never had the opportunity to have a real conversation because of that. Instead of leading from the front, he delegated task and wasn't effectively communicating with myself or others. The tension was so bad I stopped caring about the overall team goal and just focused on self. As a leader your focus is to help everyone improve and do right for the betterment of the team. He slowly not only lost my trust myself but the trust of the other team members. I ended up resigning because I wanted to leave on my own terms despite being targeted. However, the way karma had it, a few months later, I heard the company relieved him of his duties as the Director of the company. It is a necessity that you lead on ethics and do not let the power get to your head.

When you are managing a team, it is the leaders responsibility to identify strengths and weaknesses of your team and bring out the very best in each individual. You have to know how to manage egos and continue to inspire people even during the hard times. What I am saying is, it is not easy to be a leader and in order to be an effective one you must train your mind to handle all situations and especially high stressed situations. People tend to react off of emotions rather than to stop and think about the situation. Leaders can identify those situations and immediately take time to analyze situations without emotion. You are basically a firefighter day in and day out. Your job is to put out any flames or pressing issues as quickly and effectively as possible.

People speak about being a born leader, but I don't agree with that. You can have natural speaking abilities but to truly lead means you must also be coachable. In order to lead you must first be led and be willing to put others before you put yourself. Some people are not comfortable in that leadership role and that is okay, but do not take it for granted. When you are called to lead people you must act with humility and grace. These are key ingredients that keep you humble and create awareness of your ultimate goal which is to lead people.

TAKEAWAY

Practice, practice, practice is what makes perfect! But you can never be perfect when it comes to leadership or anything in life for that matter. You can only hope to continuously get better day in and day out. A true leader knows you will never be perfect so you have to always find ways to evolve and get better. For the majority of your life you have been interacting with people whether school, work or play. How you touch and change the life of a person in your interaction will define your leadership. And it always starts with gratitude; putting others before you put yourself. You want to be a leader, serve others. It is that simple, and through your grace, others will look to you as a leader. Yes, you must continue to personally develop and get better for you to reach the masses but you want to start from somewhere then apply grace to your life. Your legacy has the potential to last forever if you value what is important to you. You should always do what is in the best interest of people first before you think of self. Zig Ziglar said, “you get all you want out of life by helping others get what they want.” Or my personal favorite, “find a way to serve the many, because service to many leads to greatness.” You want to be a leader, then serve people.

Chapter Seven

Fear vs. Comfort

Until it becomes bigger than you, it will never mean as much to you

- MICHAEL DUCILLE

How hard does it have to be for you to finally say it is time to make a change? So many people are comfortable living the same way all their lives and never decide to do anything different. It is why the model of go to school and get a job to pay for school exist in the first place. It is a life with a lot less risk than betting on yourself. They say life starts at the end of your comfort zone. Let's take the cliche saying out but really analyze what that means. Take that very thing that scares you to death or makes you nervous. What does that look like for you? Public speaking, spiders, heights? The very thing that has control over your mind has control over you. I remember watching a Will Smith speech about skydiving and he speaks about fear. He explains leading up to the jump he was terrified. But until you actually make the jump, what is it that you're afraid of. You are nowhere near the airplane so why is it ruining your sleep the night before or breakfast in the morning. The thought of jumping is what caused the fear not the actual jump itself. We let nerves get the better of us in situations well before the actual event takes place. I see it all the time in people who interview for jobs, or give a speech. You cannot let fear of something, stop you from doing or achieving something.

When he actually jumped from the plane he felt complete bliss and said at the point of maximum danger is the point of minimum fear. If you can't control your mind, how do you expect to control your life? You have to push yourself to extreme limits and be comfortable overcoming it. Will Smith wraps up his speech by saying *"God placed the best things in life on the other side of fear."* But you will never know what those amazing things are if you do not confront the fears of life. You can be comfortable and miss out on those best things or you can look at fear in the face and conquer it. One of my biggest fears prepared me without knowing to become a speaker and to inspire many people.

Picture this, a 22 year old young man that could not grow facial hair and still looks like he is in high school working his first full time job as a Job Recruiter. His job was to help others find a job and give career advice. Now, imagine that same person in a room full of people that are 40+ years old doing a workshop on career readiness and how to find a job. How much credibility does that 22 year old really have in a room full of people who some have been working probably before this 22 year old was even born. I can picture that young man being terrified, feeling underqualified and getting his head chewed off because of the inexperience. That 22 year old young man was me. One of my first jobs out of college was recruiting for a company and helping people find work. Here I am giving career advice to people, and not feeling qualified to even do it. Every Wednesday, I had to go into a room of about 40-50 people and talk about career opportunities and what these individuals could do better to find employment. I remember one particular Wednesday, I was speaking about starting small and working your way up. I used the example of working at McDonald's and I said, you work your way up and as a manager you can make $45,000/year starting. And someone blurted out, I was a manager that is not true, get your facts straight. I went from feeling nervous speaking to completely embarrassed. I heard that statistic from a friend and did not research it to confirm or deny and felt stupid. The reality is, instead of posturing up and being confident, I was so nervous I froze up. According to Glassdoor, store managers at McDonald's make about 50k/year as of writing this and if I was confident in my approach I could have immediately asked him more qualifying questions. Ask him questions like were you a store manager or just a shift manager? But because I never got over my fear of public speaking my lack of confidence showed. When adversity smacked me in the face I was too scared to fight back. That gentleman literally embarrassed me in front of everyone and I immediately lost my credibility. My job was to help individuals find employment and no one trusted me to do that all because of the fear that was there. But, that was one of the best lessons that could have happened to me and I couldn't be more grateful for it.

I needed that opposition because it was the start of what failure and embarrassment looked like. For many people, experiencing that could be crippling and they'd never want to speak in public ever again. I used that experience to make sure that would never happen to me again. I said that evening walking out of work that no matter who you are or what you do, I will never let another person make me feel less than or control the situation. It was what was needed in the moment to understand that I can't shy away from moments in life. People will continue to test your abilities and if you can't step into greatness then you'll never become great. I used what happened to fuel me and get that much better in the years to come. I always had to not only be prepared for the moment but embrace the challenges that were ahead.

I want you to push yourself to confront fear in ways you never thought was possible. For some, that is skydiving out of a plane. Or it can mean speaking in front of a crowd. But you will always be limited in your belief if you don't look fear in the face and confront it. You have to speak life into all situations and not let your mind stop you from achieving what's possible. If you don't know what is possible, start reading up on other people who have achieved greatness. Unfortunately, 9 times out of 10 they were called crazy until it was actually done. They let go of limited of beliefs in their minds and from others and the sky became the limit.

TAKEAWAY

One thing I did not mention in this chapter was the fear of money. This has been something I was plagued with for a really long time because I did not have the confidence to name my price. I have a digital agency and have created well over 50+ websites for clients over the last few years and when it comes to naming a price, I would cringe up. I wanted to close every deal so I always tried to give a price I thought they could afford. I never had the confidence to look at myself as a premium brand to charge what I was worth. So I gave them a number I thought my clients would think of as a no-brainer, even as I low balled myself. I had a fear people would not pay me what I deserved because I did not think I was worth the price. And if you don't believe you are worth it then no one else will. I have personally done website work and charged $3,000 and did less work than a site I charged $400 for. The only thing that changed for me was what I knew I was worth and when that happened, people paid me accordingly. I want you to value yourself and charge what you are worth at all times. I did not value me because I was afraid but don't make the same mistake I did. I did the same work made a little more than 7 times the amount and had little to no issues with that client. We can fear many things and it typically all stems from confidence. Always confront your fears and fight it head on. Fighting fear is always better than comfort.

Chapter Eight

The Easy Route

You want something quick, put it in a microwave, but don't expect a gourmet meal from it

- Michael Ducille

I am guilty of trying to shortcut my way to success for many years. How you do one thing is how you do everything, and I have had some hard life lessons that showed me you can't fake the process. There are very rare occasions that people will just give you something without anything in return. There has to be some work or added benefit for that additional party for it to even make sense.

I remember going up to New York to visit my dad while I was still attending college in Tampa. I was stopped in Downtown Brooklyn to go shopping to get clothes to take back to Florida with me. I was on a limited budget so I tried to get all the deals. As I was passing by Dr.

Jay's in Brooklyn this guy came up to me and said I have a Dr. Jay's gift card if you want it. There's $350 on it if you'd like but I will give it to you for $150. He must have known I was a tourist and really targeted me out. Well, remember I was limited on money so anyway I could come up I said cool. I called a friend of mine and he told me to be careful there are a lot of scammers. I said he looks legit. I did not have all the cash on me at the time so I walked to the bank with him and pulled out the $150. We made the exchange close to the Dr. Jay's and when I went to the register, the card was empty. I went back out to look for the guy and he vanished into thin air.

Now I know you are looking at me like how could you get scammed like that. At any point when the mind is weak and/or desperate you will do anything to get ahead. I wasn't the first person to get scammed nor will I be the last. When you are looking for the easy route in life you will be easily manipulated to do things that are too good to be true. Understand that you have to play the long game because if you don't, it will cost you more down the road. There are never any shortcuts in life and I cannot reiterate that enough. Every time I have tried it, it never worked. The minimal work and high promise for a big financial gain. I ended up losing out on $150 and still left Downtown Brooklyn with nothing to show for it but empty pockets from a college student trying to look fly. The lesson learned was you can never get something for nothing.

Fame is another way people try and take the shortcut or the fake it till you make it approach. Athletes are some of the biggest culprits trying to take the shorter route. Steroids and other performing enhancing drugs have plagued the likes of baseball, football, mixed martial arts and many more. I look at the likes of someone like Jon 'Bones' Jones who was considered one of the best pound for pound mixed martial artist in the world. However stints with drugs and PED's have had him in and out of the octagon since 2015. I don't know if he took PED's to get a competitive advantage because he was always considered one of the best but it derailed his career. He lost a lot of his prime years dealing with suspensions and being stripped of his title multiple times.

The same things happened in the baseball era with the likes of Barry Bonds, Sammy Sosa and Mark McGwire. These were some of the best sluggers of all time and first ballot Hall of Fame worthy but to date are still trying to make it in the Hall of Fame. They used performance enhancing drugs to get a leg up on the competition and now it is costing them. They were great before it but trying to take the short cut and to extend their baseball careers ended up costing them so much more.

This microwave society that we live in because of what we see has been detrimental to people and their mental health. You look at someone's highlights and never look at their behind the scenes to see what made them. You cannot put success in a microwave for a few minutes, warm it up and expect a great meal. Ask yourself if you prefer a tv dinner over a home cooked meal and that should put things into perspective for you. Don't use social media as a way to define a timetable for success or how quickly it takes. Colonel Sanders didn't found KFC until his 60's and didn't sell his franchise until he was 73 years old. Now KFC is one of the largest fast food chains in the world. But if Instagram was around and you see the Founder of KFC hanging out on the beach and living the life, you would have no idea that he contemplated suicide or got turned down when he tried to franchise his recipe over 1000 times. He said, *"I made a resolve then that I was going to amount to something if I could. And no hours, nor amount of labor, nor amount of money would deter me from giving the best that there was in me."*

That is all you can ask of yourself. Give it the very best you have no matter the circumstance. Don't let anyone or anything deter you from your goals. And most importantly, don't cheat success, you will have to put in the man hours no matter what, so you might as well start now. Study the greats, match their hustle, and trust the process.

TAKEAWAY

Do not cheat the process ever! The story of the chinese bamboo tree is quite simple. Just like any other plant, you water, fertilize and give it light. What makes this plant different is for the first five years you see no visible growth. You are putting in the same work day in and day out and see no results yet. And if you stop doing the daily things like watering this plant it will die before you ever see it sprout. After the 5th year it can grow up to 80 feet in just six weeks time. The hard work of watering and taking care of this tree resulted in massive growth in six weeks. But what you did not see if the growth underneath the ground. When you are working for a goal you won't see results right away. You are working internally and no one can see the inside of you that is growing. You couldn't see this roots underneath the soil growing on that bamboo tree so do not expect anyone else to see what is growing inside of you. But the patience and diligence allowed this tree to reach its full potential. You can not take the easy route to success. In order for you to build a solid foundation you have to give yourself time to lay the bricks down correctly. There are certain things that require time and dedication for it to stand tall through the test of time. The Egyptian pyramids are a great example because it took twenty years to build one of the seven wonders of the world. At any point if the workers tried to rush or take the easy route I can almost guarantee it wouldn't still be standing. There is no elevator to success, you have to take the stairs.

Chapter Nine

Social Media

Social media. Control it, don't let it control you.

- Michael Ducille

According to Statista, In 2017, roughly eighty percent of the U.S. population had a social media profile. The increased usage and of social media is expected to rise. This shows me how powerful social media is and how it manipulates our mind. According to The Economist roughly 63% of people on Instagram reported that they were miserable and they spend about an hour on that platform per day. I am giving you these statistics to show how powerful yet dangerous social media can be if not used in a controlled state. We are using our devices to step away from reality into fantasy to seek comfort from a place we shouldn't. But who do we blame for this? Where exactly does this addiction lie?

When you engage in social media it releases a chemical in our brains called dopamine. Dopamine is a chemical transmitter in the brain that sends signals to the central nervous system. It is most commonly recognized for the role it plays in motivation, rewards, and pleasure. This is what makes us feel good when we post a picture and get a bunch of likes and comments. Social media addiction is compared to alcohol by some because it is the same chemical that makes you feel good when you drink. It is highly addictive. It has become an addiction to where you fall into a rabbit hole of videos and meaningless pictures online. You use it to compare yourself with other people. And you follow the lives of other people and live your life vicariously through them. You go on your device to check the weather and end up on social media for 30 minutes looking at things that don't matter from people who don't care about you or know you exist. I've been out with friends and would look at my cell phone and scroll through a newsfeed just because. Or it felt like something to do when there was no clear direction. I was in a wedding and walked down the aisle and looked over at someone scrolling through their feed. As something as sacred as a wedding we give more attention to the fantasy of social media than the reality of what is there.

Sean Parker, former President of Facebook said in an interview, "it's a social validation feedback loop. Exactly the kind of thing that hackers like myself come up with, because you're exploiting a vulnerability in human psychology." They give you that hit of dopamine to increase morale and make you feel good about yourself based on the engagement you receive. Understanding that social media is used to make you addicted, you have to find ways to outsmart them. I almost felt like it was an addiction that I could not break. So I had to take steps to make sure that I wasn't being psychology controlled by it.

I started to become self-aware that even when I did not want to, I would end up on social media just because it was habitual. What I ended up doing was taking a social media break because just like a recovering alcoholic or gambler, I had to stay away from it altogether. At first I tried to limit myself from using social media to only once per day but that did not work for me. I still ended up clicking on the app subconsciously. I had to delete all the apps off of my phone and have a friend change my password because I did not trust myself to not go on. I had to remove myself from the situation completely. Are you willing to remove yourself from the very thing you are addicted to for the advancement of your growth? I vowed for 30 days not to touch it for personal growth. I wanted to test this 'addiction' that I had and find out if it would mentally break me. If things like fear of missing out bothered me or not being able to ideally scroll down a newsfeed to pass the time. And really starting to become very present in the moment and what was in front of me. I had to get really good at being of my word. Once the time allotted I realized

I wasn't addicted at all and it was more of a habit that I had to control. We aren't born scrolling on Instagram or Facebook. You don't come out of the womb smoking or drinking. These are social norms that you eventually become addicted to. If you can break those social norms then you can start living again and getting reacquainted with myself and the people around me.

We've become so addicted to social media and devices that we stop forming meaningful relationships with people. We use the internet to try and form this persona of who we want people to think we are rather than who we actually are. This is why studies have shown that people who spend more time on social media tend to be more depressed than those who don't spend as much. They know it feels good when we get likes and comments so it forces us to keep sharing and adding content. But now we forget who we've really become and how to interact with people. Look at the popularity of the dating app Tinder. Now everyone is anxious to swipe left or right to find that next great person. We've built so much online confidence that we forgot how to have real conversations in person. It has become normal to do online dating and according to eharmony the dating website, they claim they are responsible for 4% of all marriages in the U.S. Not to mention the millions of users that are on all dating sites across the country. However, almost 50% of marriages end up in divorce or separation. I am not blaming dating websites for this but what I am saying is it takes working on yourself and forming real relationships on a daily basis. This persona you put online for other people will eventually wear off when it comes time to be face to face. And even when that does happen, it takes even more work to sustain a level of excellence and trust. Don't let what others do online determine the success you have. Don't compare your behind the scenes, to someone else's highlight reel they show online.

I am not telling you to get off social media or online, but what I am saying is sometimes a break is needed. We know that people who spend more time on social media suffer higher rates of depression and anxiety. If we know this information, what keeps us on there so long and why can't we break the habit? Stop living life vicariously through other people and start living your own life. Hoping and wishing your situation will change because you looked at someone else living what they portray as a great life does nothing for you. If you can't monitor your activity then it is imperative to stay away for some time. You cannot manage what you don't measure. The world will go on and don't worry, you won't be missing anything important.

TAKEAWAY:

Here is another self-assessment that you will have to take of yourself. Do you look at social media and compare your life to what you see people doing online?

I thought by this age I would have had my stuff together already and I do not. How can I accelerate my life to be like this person I saw on social media? You get in this rabbit hole of looking at so many other people and you stop focusing on yourself and being the best version of you. Competition does not exist when you are focusing on you. If you're unhappy with your life right now it is your responsibility to change it. When you waste time looking at what others have done it becomes wasted energy. If you are struggling with how you feel or distractions because of social media, GET OFF OF IT. It might seem like an addiction but once you step away from it you step back into reality. Everyone is going through something despite what they may put on social media. If you have a problem separating social media from reality then you need to step away from it completely.

Chapter Ten

Perspective

"The only thing you sometimes have control over is perspective. You don't have control over your situation. But you have a choice about how you view it."

- Chris Pine

Life is about perspective. I am sure you've heard the common phrase, glass half full not half empty. The meaning behind that quote is seeing things positively not negatively. Really embracing what is ahead not looking at what is behind. Let me be real with you. Life will always suck if you choose to let it. This book is big on mindset because it is a perspective shift that allows you to see things differently. The 1 Percent Mindset takes away all the excuses of life and puts you in a position to do impossible things when people say it isn't possible. Life will start to show up in areas of your life based on how you view things. I spoke to you about one of my mentors Matthew Pitts in an earlier chapter and he told me a story that will always resonate with me.

The story is about two twin boys who grew up in poverty and had every excuse why they could not be successful. When they interviewed the first twin he said it was because my parents didn't love me. I went to a bad school. There was crime everywhere. I grew up on the wrong side of the tracks. I had no real direction and my environment molded me to the person I am. That is why I am not successful. They interviewed the other twin and he said it was because my parents didn't love me. I went to a bad school. There was crime everywhere. I grew up on the wrong side of the tracks. I had no real direction and my environment molded me to the person I am. That is why I am SUCCESSFUL. Two brothers grew up in the same environment but had different perspectives on life. One used it as an excuse for his outcome and the other used it as fuel to determine his outcome. You don't have control of the hand you are dealt growing up, but you can determine how you play those cards.

When life punches you in the face always remember the target. You are not excused from tough times and you are not the only one going through it. Life doesn't target you and make everyone else immune to discomfort. So when you are throwing darts and blaming people for why things aren't the way it should be, make sure you hit the target of the problem. No outside factor but you can determine your perspective and if you do not see that then you will always be a victim. Drake, famous rapper said, "live in the same building but we have different views." And that means it's your way of being that needs to be fixed. You can't look at anything from a single lens because there are always many ways to see the same thing. I remember a situation in particular where I greeted a former classmate of mine and she completely ignored me.

For the rest of the school year I completely ignored, spoke about, and disrespected her because of what she did to me. In my head I said, if she can do this, then she doesn't deserve my respect at all. I decided to reach out to her later on in the year and found out after that on that particular day she lost a close friend and she was out of it. It wasn't intentional but from my vintage point I felt disrespected. Here I was, harboring all of this negative energy in my little body for months at a time for no reason at all. Meanwhile, she is living her life not even thinking about that one situation I was holding onto. Instead of saying in my head, she ignored me, I should be thinking what she's going through right now to be dismissive. I made it about me and my feelings. When you start to make things about you, you will never have perspective on any view but your own.

I challenge you to view the way you look at things in your life currently. Are you making excuses as to why you are in your situation? Or are you using it as fuel to be inspired and motivated? Which brother are you? Henry Ford said whether you think you can or can't, you're right. Don't let someone's disbelief and your perspective determine your outcome.

Roger Bannister is most known for being the first person to break 4 minutes running a mile. Prior to him running it in less than 4 minutes, experts said the human body wasn't capable of running a mile in less than 4 minutes. He turned the impossible and made it possible and that 4 minute mile, which experts said could never happen, was broken many times thereafter. Don't let people's beliefs limit your view on what is possible for you.

TAKEAWAY

The thing that is more important than energy and time is perspective. We need to understand there are people out there that have it far worse than you and are crushing it right now. Quite frankly, they are making your excuses look absolutely pathetic. No one cares that your dog died or your arm hurts. If you use personal pain or discomfort to cripple you, you start to look silly when someone with no arms at all is doing amazing things. If you go by this philosophy I was taught long ago then you can look at life different. I was told never get too high on the high's, or too low on the low's. Life is like the stock market, there will be ups and downs every single day. You can not let emotion control you in any particular direction. You take what life gives you and you adjust accordingly. You understand that someone will always have it worse than you do so you can get through anything. You start off your day by making a declaration on what you want for yourself. Mine goes something like this:

I declare peace

I declare abundance in my life

I expect clarity and happiness

I will reject any negativity that comes my way

I am thankful for all I have

I will be a blessing to others

Chapter Eleven

You vs. You

The minute I started taking myself seriously is when others started taking me seriously.

- Mark Clennon

The biggest battle we have against ourselves is our minds. One of my biggest accomplishments to date was the release of my motivational album The 1 Percent Mindset Presents: You vs You. Before I dive into some of the tracks and what they mean I want to take you behind the scenes. You vs You means so much because if at any point your mind defeats you, then you lose. The battle against yourself is hard, so let me tell you how this album even started. My coach Anthony challenged me to create because of my ability to speak and move people. I was never a musically inclined or even considered myself much of a writer. What I could do was speak from truth and my experiences, so we set a deadline for 2 months out to produce a motivational album that the world could be inspired by. I started to listen to other motivational speakers' albums and fell in love with Inky Johnson's Empty the Bucket album. It inspired me because he told his story and spoke from truth. Inky Johnson was an All-Pro Defensive Back in college and recognized as a projected top 30 draft pick. He would be an automatic millionaire once he completed his senior season at the University of Tennessee. In one of his final games he did what was routine for him. He went for a tackle and sustained an injury to his nerves and blood vessels and became paralyzed on his right side. He had 8 games left and never cheated the process. He details so many inspirational and motivating moments within that album and I knew if I could provide just half the value I received from that album then people would love it.

My coach Anthony and I set the date to May 7th, 2018 and decided to do a promo run for 5 weeks releasing snippets to prepare for this album. Preparation is the cornerstone of success and if you fail to plan, you plan to fail. About three weeks before the album was supposed to be released, I drove from New York City to Boston to record the album at a friend's house who volunteered his time and his beats for me. The plan was to leave New York around 6am to get there around 10am. On the way driving to Boston, my car overheats and stuck on the side of the road for about 30 minutes. I end up at a mechanic and spend another 2+ hours there. I didn't end up getting to my destination until about 3pm and had to leave by 7pm to head back to New York.

I spoke about preparation because up until that point, anytime I spoke or did any videos it was always off the top of my head. I never wrote anything down or rehearsed. I felt like the Lil' Wayne of motivational speaking because I never wrote I just flowed. However, on that day it was different. I had the beat playing in the background but I could not catch the beat and speak articulately at the same time. Within those 4 hours I completed one, maybe two songs. I didn't prepare and I thought I could just wing it. I am two weeks out from my scheduled release date and I have two half finished tracks. Lack of planning forced me to go back to Boston the very next weekend to try and get everything completed within those few hours again. This go around I was better prepared. I knocked out about 6 songs that I had prewritten and felt pretty good. However, it was crunch time and because I waited so long the tracks couldn't get engineered and produced in time to make the release date. The entire time I was pushing this May 7th date on all of my social media platforms and it wasn't going to get released in time. So to improvise, I created a 'Making of the Album' documentary to show the behind the scenes of what it looked like to create an album from start to finish. It was important that I released something on May 7th. Yes, I did not make the deadline and no one knew it was an album I was releasing but putting something out there for my supporters was important. After the release of the documentary I put my head down and recorded 3 more tracks from New York and made the track total up to 11. I spent about 3 hours going over the album with trusted advisors and it was finally ready for release. Can I be honest and tell you that even at that point I hated the album. It was then I realized that nothing will ever be perfect to the creator. You will always feel like you can do better. So with lots of hesitation, I submitted the album for release.

On May 28th, The 1 Percent Mindset Presents: You vs. You was released on all major streaming platforms. My first motivational album was completed and now it was time to get feedback from the people. The beauty of this project was everything I spoke about came from a perspective of a truth that I lived. And when speaking to people, everyone had a different favorite track that resonated with them. I spoke about topics that everyone could relate and someone went through a similar experience. Before I talk about a few tracks I want to show you a tracklist

The 1 Percent Mindset Presents You vs. You by Michael Ducille

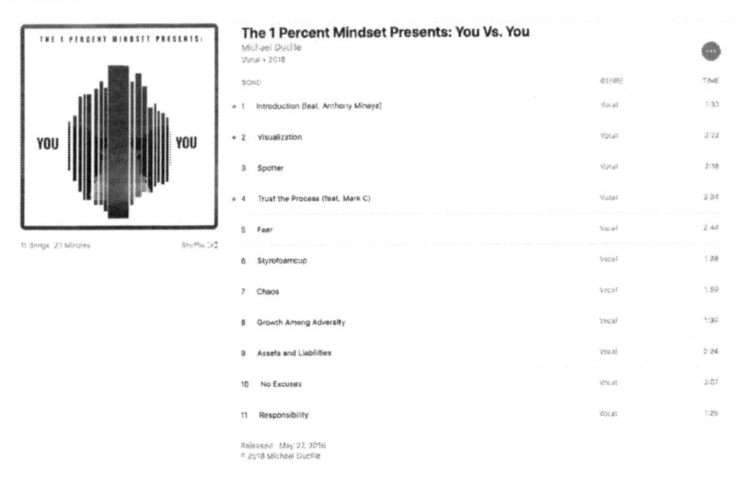

This 11 track album impacted and inspired not only myself but so many other people. I could break down track by track but I want to go over my mindset creating this album and where the inspiration came from. One of my favorite tracks is Spotter and it is about having someone who can hold you accountable and push you to achieve more. On this track I speak about being in the gym. Typically when you are trying to max out (lift, push, or pull more than you ever have) you need someone there to spot you to make sure they have your back just in case you think you can not do it. This track was inspired by my personal spotter at the gym. I was doing squats and at one point I felt I could not squat anymore. He was in my ear and telling to not give up, and I had a few more left. When I am struggling the most, he is there to push and inspire me to keep going or even give some assistance. In life you need a person that will get you out of that funk and push you to achieve more. No one makes it on their own. You can have a drive, or an inspiration but success is never predicated just on self. When you have the right people around you or inspired by greatness, it takes you to a level you couldn't get to just on your own.

My point is to have a spotter with you that aligns with your goals and dreams is crucial. As you continue to surround yourself with those people, you have no choice but to elevate. I worked out with people who were bigger than I was (easy to do at 135lbs) because it gave me something to push for. My goal was to gain weight and I added almost 20lbs of muscle within my first 6-8 months.

But your spotter doesn't just have to be fitness based. What fitness did for me was added confidence in so many other areas of my life. I can go into any business meeting with the confidence that I will close any deal or nail any interview. The reason is in my mind. I look at the other person not only as equal regardless of their position or title; but in my head, they don't work as hard as I do. They aren't waking up at 4:30 am every morning to go to the gym. They aren't forced to perform at a high level mentally and physically day in and day out. Quite frankly, they might be but in my mind because of the work I put in daily, I go in with that confidence. I win the battle against my mind before I do anything else.

So I go into every situation with the utmost confidence because of the confidence I have in myself. You gain that confidence through personal development both physically and mentally. I remember teaching a class about how to nail an interview and the first thing I noticed when doing mock interviews were how nervous everyone was. When asking a simple question like tell me a little about yourself and your work experience it would make some tense up. I then asked one simple question to change the perspective of the class. If it was your child or peer asking you the same question would you still feel nervous? Everyone said no they wouldn't. Well why does another human being allow you to tense up? I'm not saying interviews can't be tough but I noticed a lot of them wouldn't get the job before they even said one word out their mouth. You have to find ways to pump yourself up and build confidence. The gym was my outlet and having a spotter allowed me to push myself to limits I thought was never possible. And how you do one thing is how you do everything. I utilize that same push to reach my peak in all areas of life.

What doesn't kill you makes you stronger is what they say. So when I was writing Growth Among Adversity, another track off the album, I thought about how much people learn through pain. It is through that adversity that forces you to grow. In this track I tell a story about a gentleman who kept throwing trash into his neighbor's yard. Eventually, that neighbor ended up growing beautiful flowers utilizing the garbage the man through to fertilize the soil. We can sometimes be so quick to react to the negative that we don't take the time to see if there are any lessons to be learned, or any possible gems that can be taken from the situation. This person had every right to be upset that garbage was in their yard daily. Instead, they figured out a way to grow beautiful flowers that even had the man in awe. People will always try and find a way to burn down your building instead of building their own. Life is about adjustments and it is necessary to assess a situation before reacting negatively to it. Life is what you make it and if you think it sucks, then it will. But if you can use the adversity to fuel you then the potential for growth will always be there.

TAKEAWAY

I will keep this brief! Go buy/stream the album on whatever platform you listen to music. I put together all of my experiences and the experiences of others to create a project to inspire. Everyone resonates with a different track because we all have something we are internally battling on a daily basis. So, stop what you are doing right now and listen to the tracks. Leave feedback and let me know what you think.

Chapter Twelve

Truth

The truth hurts, then you get over it

- Michael Ducille

It's almost comical how we hammer it into children that they should always tell the truth, yet majority of adults lie on a daily basis. Lying makes us feel comfortable; it's the veil between ourselves and the consequences we fear will come with transparency. There are plenty of instances in which I chose to wrap myself in the comfort of my lies to avoid reality, and it turned out in my favor... at least I thought it did.

However, despite the lies that I told to keep myself 'safe', or the lies others told me trying to spare me from whatever they felt I couldn't handle, it was once I recognized that actually being honest was the most transformative experience for me. When they say that, "the truth shall set you free", it's not always in the literal sense— in fact there are some truths that will probably get you locked up. However, acknowledging the truth about myself, allowed me to see life differently.

For starters, if we're being quite honest, the truth is I never expected to write a book, let alone finish one. I never believed that I could not only complete a motivational album, but that people would actually WANT to listen to it. The truth is, I masked my pain with smiles and laughter so much that the world never knew the true pain I was experiencing. Hell, I looked like I didn't have a care in the world to outsiders, despite being in some of the darkest spaces of my life. The truth is, there were many times where I lacked confidence and felt lost. It wasn't until I was able to live in my own truth and acknowledge where I was, that I was able to change the course of my life. First within myself, and then in every other aspect of my life. I recognized that the 'freedom' I sought out, was one where I broke the very chains I had placed on myself. I always tried to keep up with Joneses because they seemed to have everything perfect and who doesn't want to live a perfect life. What I did a terrible job at was owning my truth. I wanted to appear to be a superhero to everyone and wasn't mentally strong enough to show my weaknesses and insecurities. I hid from my own reality thus living in a fantasy world that I couldn't keep up with. At some point I had to look in the mirror and say it was okay to get help, or speak to someone. It was okay to be vulnerable and seek help where necessary.

I had to realize I was easily distracted and sometimes I wasn't practicing what I was preaching. I had to come to realization that I wasn't getting the results I wanted because I didn't put in the proper work. I said at the beginning of this book that in order to be elite in any area you can not cheat the process. It is the work you put in day in and day out that will determine the level of success that you have.

The 1 Percent Mindset is all about doing what 99% of the other people won't do. It is raising your level of productivity so high that no one else can compete with you. There is no magic pill for success. Hard work beats talent when talent doesn't work hard. And a lot of times you have to outwill the next person to be the very best. How bad do you want it isn't a question you have to ask someone elite. You know they already want it and will do anything in their power to get it. The reason you lose friends in the process is because you have to go into isolation mode. You don't have the luxury to go out and party and take days off when there is work to accomplish and things you have to get done. So when the road gets tough, you don't think about quitting because you've invested so much that it becomes hard to just give up. You don't want to let yourself down but more importantly, you don't want to let the people around you that you care about down. It almost feels like you have no choice but to succeed. You change your mindset because you expect to go through obstacles, personally develop, get better but most importantly, make an impact. Everyone with success has a story. They had to have The 1 Percent Mindset to make it. The question now is, what is your story? What are you willing to go through to make it? In the process, do you plan on living your truth along the way? There is no such thing as fake it till you make it. Success isn't a lottery ticket that you can just win without work. It takes time and you have to have discipline and patience along the way. Surround yourself with the right people and always remember; The 1 Percent: It's A Mindset.

TAKEAWAY

As you wrap up the end of this book, know that The 1 Percent Mindset isn't easily attained. But more than half the battle starts if you can control your mind and the destiny you have for yourself. You want something, go after it, figure it out, but don't quit. As long as you keep making progress and you are not staying stagnant you should be proud of yourself. The truth is I am still in a battle of wanting to do more and thinking I should be further ahead. But someone put things into perspective for me that changed things. In December 2017, The 1 Percent Mindset was born; May 2018, The 1 Percent Mindset Presents: You vs. You was released. And now, my final words in this book will be completed November of 2018. I released a motivational album and wrote a book all within a years' time with so much more in store. I stopped comparing myself to everyone else and started becoming proud of my accomplishments at hand. I hope this takeaway allows you to see that the truth is... you are already great. All you must do now, is tap into it.

About The Author

Michael Ducille, Jr. is a graduate from the University of South Florida and a millennial entrepreneur that specializes in youth development and training. He got his start in entrepreneurship starting a website consultation business that he scaled quickly with zero capital. Shortly after, he started studying created The 1 Percent Mindset platform after creating multiple videos on motivation and mindset. Also, released his first motivational album You vs. You in May of 2018. He has a passion for working with young people and recently partnered with a company to bring youth entrepreneurship to New York City. He lives by the quote, “you get all you want out of life by helping others get what they want” by Zig Ziglar.

Acknowledgements

There are so many people I would like to thank for helping me complete this book and keeping me on track. First and foremost I want to thank God for setting me up with all the right people who motivated and inspired me to write and complete this book. I always told myself I wasn't a writer and now I have a published book. It is still very surreal to me at times. I would like to send a big shout out to my friend Kristine who spent countless hours reviewing and editing this book. She was willing to transcribe the entire book for me without me writing a single word if I let her. So I truly appreciate your friendship and what you helped me create. I want to thank my beautiful mother for taking the time to edit the majority of this book while being on a hard deadline to finish it. I want to thank Stephanie for allowing all facets of The 1 Percent Mindset to actually function on a day in and day out basis, you are truly appreciated. And want to thank the rest of my team who researched, advised, reviewed, or offered any kind of support with the creation of this book. The goal is to impact and inspire thousands and possibly millions of people. For the very first book, I think we can accomplish that goal.